D0793819

The Rose
Rose
in the
Garden

Kelly Doudna

ABDO
Publishing Company

THIS BOOK IS THE PROPERTY OF
THE NATIONAL CITY PUBLIC LIBRARY
CHILDREN'S BOOK

Published by SandCastle™, an imprint of ABDO Publishing Company, 4940 Viking Drive, Edina, Minnesota 55435.

Copyright © 2002 by Abdo Consulting Group, Inc. International copyrights reserved in all countries. No part of this book may be reproduced in any form without written permission from the publisher. SandCastle™ is a trademark and logo of Abdo Publishing Company.

Printed in the United States.

Photo credits: Corbis Images, Digital Vision, Eyewire Images, PhotoDisc, Rubberball Productions

Library of Congress Cataloging-in-Publication Data

Doudna, Kelly, 1963-
    The rose rose in the garden / Kelly Doudna.
      p. cm. -- (Homonyms)
    Includes index.
    Summary: Photographs and simple text introduce homonyms, words that are spelled and sound the same but have different meanings.
    ISBN 1-57765-789-6
      1. English language--Homonyms--Juvenile literature. [1. English language--Homonyms.] I. Title.

PE1595 .D77 2002
428.1--dc21

                                                      2001053312

The SandCastle concept, content, and reading method have been reviewed and approved by a national advisory board including literacy specialists, librarians, elementary school teachers, early childhood education professionals, and parents.

Let Us Know

After reading the book, SandCastle would like you to tell us your stories about reading. What is your favorite page? Was there something hard that you needed help with? Share the ups and downs of learning to read. We want to hear from you! To get posted on the Abdo Publishing Company Web site, send us email at:

sandcastle@abdopub.com

About SandCastle™
Nonfiction books for the beginning reader

- Basic concepts of phonics are incorporated with integrated language methods of reading instruction. Most words are short, and phrases, letter sounds, and word sounds are repeated.

- Book levels are based on the ATOS™ for Books formula. Other considerations for readability include the number of words in each sentence, the number of characters in each word, and word lists based on curriculum frameworks.

- Full-color photography reinforces word meanings and concepts.

- "Words I Can Read" list at the end of each book teaches basic elements of grammar, helps the reader recognize the words in the text, and builds vocabulary.

- Reading levels are indicated by the number of flags on the castle.

SandCastle uses the following definitions for this series:

- Homographs: words that are spelled the same but sound different and have different meanings. *Easy memory tip: "-graph"= same look*

- Homonyms: words that are spelled and sound the same but have different meanings. *Easy memory tip: "-nym"= same name*

- Homophones: words that sound alike but are spelled differently and have different meanings. *Easy memory tip: "-phone"= sound alike*

Look for more SandCastle books in these three reading levels:

Level 1 (one flag)	**Level 2** (two flags)	**Level 3** (three flags)

Grades Pre-K to K 5 or fewer words per page	**Grades K to 1** 5 to 10 words per page	**Grades 1 to 2** 10 to 15 words per page

note   note

Homonyms are words that are spelled and sound the same but have different meanings.

This duck has six ducklings.

She leads them around the farm.

I must **duck** down when I go through the door of the playhouse.

There are a lot of cars.

My school bus is stuck in the traffic jam.

It is time for lunch.

We make peanut butter and jam sandwiches.

This kangaroo lives in Australia.

It has long legs and is a good jumper.

Sometimes I like to wear a dress.

Today I am wearing a blue jumper.

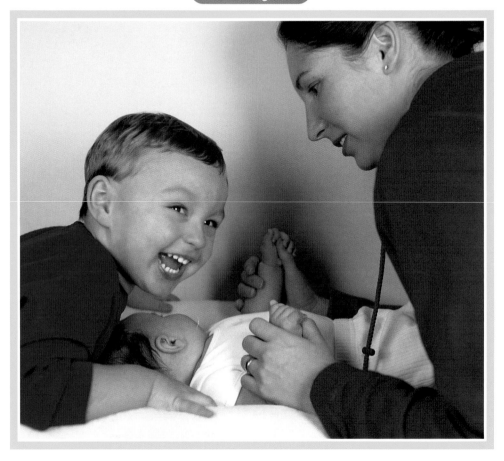

I love my baby sister.

I get a kick out of helping Mom with her.

I want to play soccer.

I am learning how to kick the ball.

I am nice to my puppies.

I feel good when I am **kind** to animals.

I have strawberry ice cream.

Next time I will have a different kind.

We are noisy in music class.

We make a loud racket.

I got a new tennis racket.

I hope it will help me play well.

I am very tired.

Grandma holds me while I rest.

I shucked one ear of corn.

I still have to shuck the rest of them.

I am almost three feet tall.

Three feet equals one yard.

I enjoy being outside in the summer.

Where do I like to lie?

(yard)

Words I Can Read

Nouns

A noun is a person, place, or thing

animals (AN-uh-muhlz)
  p. 14
ball (BAWL) p. 13
cars (KARZ) p. 8
corn (KORN) p. 19
door (DOR) p. 7
dress (DRESS) p. 11
duck (DUHK) p. 6
ducklings (DUHK-lingz)
  p. 6
ear (IHR) p. 19
farm (FARM) p. 6
feet (FEET) p. 20
homonyms
  (HOM-uh-nimz) p. 5
ice cream
  (EYESS KREEM) p. 15
jam (JAM) p. 9
jumper (JUHM-pur)
  pp. 10, 11

kangaroo
  (kang-guh-ROO) p. 10
kick (KIK) p. 12
kind (KINDE) p. 15
legs (LEGZ) p. 10
lot (LOT) p. 8
lunch (LUHNCH) p. 9
meanings (MEE-ningz)
  p. 5
music class
  (MYOO-zik KLASS)
  p. 16
note (NOHT) p. 4
peanut butter
  (PEE-nuht BUHT-ur)
  p. 9
playhouse
  (PLAY-houss) p. 7
puppies (PUHP-eez)
  p. 14

racket (RAK-it) p. 16
rest (REST) p. 19
sandwiches
  (SAND-wich-ez) p. 9
school bus
  (SKOOL BUHSS) p. 8
sister (SISS-tur) p. 12
soccer (SOK-ur) p. 13
summer (SUHM-ur) p. 21
tennis racket
  (TEN-iss RAK-it) p. 17
time (TIME) pp. 9, 15
today (tuh-DAY) p. 11
traffic jam
  (TRAF-ik JAM) p. 8
words (WURDZ) p. 5
yard (YARD) pp. 20, 21

Proper Nouns

A proper noun is the name of a
person, place, or thing

Australia
  (aw-STRAYL-yuh)
  p. 10

Grandma
  (GRAND-mah) p. 18

Mom (MOM) p. 12

Pronouns

A pronoun is a word that replaces a noun

her (HUR) p. 12

I (EYE) pp. 7, 11, 12, 13, 14, 15, 17, 18, 19, 20, 21

it (IT) pp. 9, 10, 17

me (MEE) pp. 17, 18

she (SHEE) p. 6

that (THAT) p. 5

them (THEM) pp. 6, 19

there (THAIR) p. 8

we (WEE) pp. 9, 16

Verbs

A verb is an action or being word

am (AM) pp. 11, 13, 14, 18, 20

are (AR) pp. 5, 8, 16

being (BEE-ing) p. 21

do (DOO) p. 21

duck (DUHK) p. 7

enjoy (en-JOI) p. 21

equals (EE-kwuhlz) p. 20

feel (FEEL) p. 14

get (GET) p. 12

go (GOH) p. 7

got (GOT) p. 17

has (HAZ) pp. 6, 10

have (HAV) pp. 5, 15, 19

help (HELP) p. 17

helping (HELP-ing) p. 12

holds (HOHLDZ) p. 18

hope (HOPE) p. 17

is (IZ) pp. 8, 9, 10

kick (KIK) p. 13

leads (LEEDZ) p. 6

learning (LURN-ing) p. 13

lie (LYE) p. 21

like (LIKE) pp. 11, 21

lives (LIVZ) p. 10

love (LUHV) p. 12

make (MAYK) pp. 9, 16

must (MUHST) p. 7

play (PLAY) pp. 13, 17

rest (REST) p. 18

shuck (SHUHK) p. 19

shucked (SHUHKT) p. 19

sound (SOUND) p. 5

spelled (SPELD) p. 5

stuck (STUHK) p. 8

want (WONT) p. 13

wear (WAIR) p. 11

wearing (WAIR-ing) p. 11

will (WIL) pp. 15, 17

23

Adjectives

An adjective describes something

baby (BAY-bee) p. 12
blue (BLOO) p. 11
different (DIF-ur-uhnt)
  pp. 5, 15
good (gud) pp. 10, 14
kind (KINDE) p. 14
long (LAWNG) p. 10
loud (LOUD) p. 16

my (MYE) pp. 8, 12, 14
new (NOO) p. 17
next (NEKST) p. 15
nice (NEYESS) p. 14
noisy (NOI-zee) p. 16
one (WUHN) pp. 19, 20
same (SAYM) p. 5

six (SIKS) p. 6
strawberry
  (STRAW-ber-ee) p. 15
tall (TAWL) p. 20
this (THISS) pp. 6, 10
three (THREE) p. 20
tired (TIRED) p. 18

Adverbs

An adverb tells how, when, or where
something happens

almost (AWL-most) p. 20
down (DOUN) p. 7
out (OUT) p. 12
outside (out-SIDE) p. 21

sometimes
  (SUHM-timez) p. 11
still (STIL) p. 19

very (VER-ee) p. 18
well (WEL) p. 17
where (WAIR) p. 21

The
AR Bookfinder
rating for
this book is

Book Level:

AR Points: